FOCUS ON
INDIA

Shahrukh Husain

Evans Brothers Limited

For Monty and Samira

Published by Evans Brothers Limited
2A Portman Mansions
Chiltern Street
London W1M 1LE

First published in Great Britain in 1986 by
Hamish Hamilton Children's Books

© Shahrukh Husain 1986

First published 1986
New edition published 1991
Reprinted 1993, 1994, 1997

Design by Andrew Shoolbred
Map by Tony Garrett
Illustrations by Martin Ursell

Printed in Spain by GRAFO, S.A. – Bilbao

ISBN 0 237 60185 0

Acknowledgements
The author and publishers would like to thank the following for permission
to reproduce the photographs: All Sport 17; Arul & Jogi Somaya, Compix
13 (bottom); Greg Evans 6 (left), 22 (left); Susan Griggs Agency 19 (left),
25 (bottom), 31 (top); Robert Harding Picture Library 6 (right), 7, 8 (right),
9, 12 (right), 13 (top), 14, 15, 18, 20, 21 22 (right), J. Nov 23, 24, 25 (top),
27, 29 (top), 30, 31 (left), Liba Taylor, Hutchison Library 26; Navketan,
courtesy of Hyphen Films 16; Images Colour Library 29 (bottom); Panos
Pictures 10; Photographers' Library title page, contents page 10 (right), 11,
19 (top), 28.

Cover Saris, the national costume of Indian women,
vary in style from district to district.

Title page Desert travellers near the Pakistan border.

Opposite Dawn comes up over the Ganges at Varanasi.

Contents

Introducing India

India is the seventh largest country in the world. Its Indian name is Bharat. Nearly 850 million people live here, making its population the second highest in the world. Nearly 36% are children below the age of fifteen! It covers an area of 3,287,782 square kilometres – the same size as all the European countries put together, with the exception of Russia. There are sixteen official languages in India and twenty-two states. Hindu is the official language of six states. Each state has its own governor but certain parts of India, such as the capital Delhi, the islands and the far-flung border areas, are under the rule of central government. These areas are called Union Territories. Nineteen kilometres (12 nautical miles) of the surrounding sea is also Indian territory.

Country of contrast

Because India is so large, it is a country of great contrasts. It can be divided into four main areas – the mountain ranges, the Ganges plains, the desert and the southern peninsula. In the north-west lies the enormous Thar desert and the city of Jaisalmer in Rajasthan, which has only 5 centimetres of rain a year. Sometimes it does not rain at all. On the other hand, Cherrapunji in the Meghalayas has the highest rainfall in the world at about 1080 centimetres a year. More than 3 centimetres of rain can fall in five minutes. The Himalayan mountains are so cold and barren that hardly anyone lives in the higher parts, but the Nilgiri mountains of South India are perfect for living in. The climate is temperate and the soil fertile.

The people

Indians belong to many different physical types. The people from Kashmir in the northern mountains are tall with light skins and pale eyes. Often they have golden-brown hair. The poor often live on houseboats moored to the banks of the famous lakes.

Farther up towards the Tibetan border, in Ladakh and Leh, the people are small, with the high cheek-bones of their neighbours in Tibet and China. They have to be very hardy to survive the tough living conditions. The weather is cold and the rocky soil does not allow much food to grow.

The people of Punjab are well-built, vigorous people. They have many advantages – fertile soil, a pleasant climate and an abundant water supply, which comes from the five rivers which flow through their land.

In the south and in Bengal, where the sun is strongest, people tend to be dark-skinned. The women are known for their beautiful hair and eyes. Village homes are made from wood, straw, mud or brick. Many live by water and make their living from fishing, freighting or ferrying.

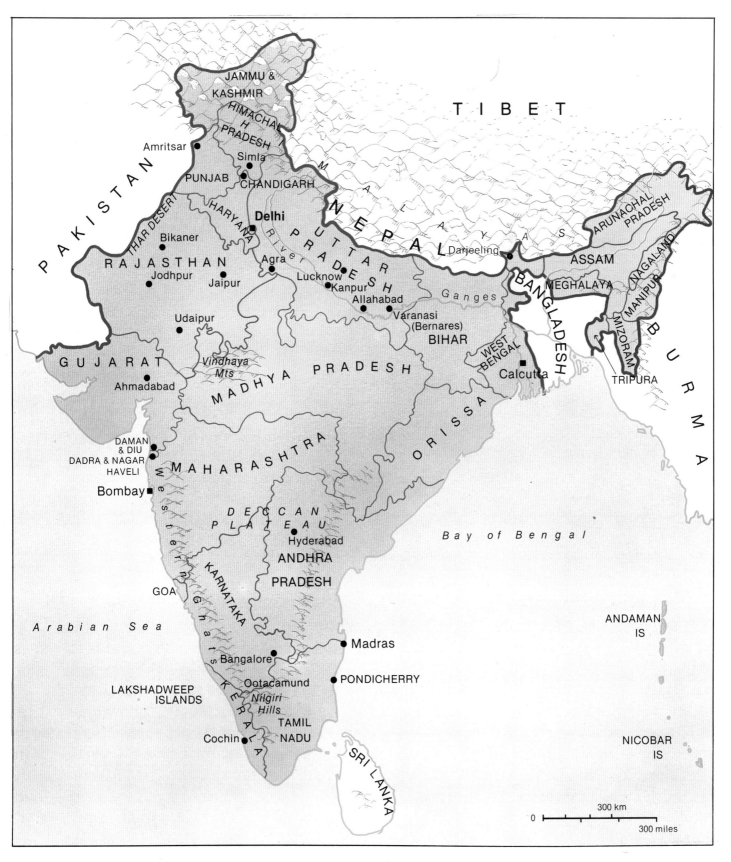

TIBET

JAMMU &
KASHMIR

HIMACHAL
PRADESH

Amritsar

Simla

PUNJAB

CHANDIGARH

PAKISTAN

THAR DESERT

HARYANA

Delhi

Bikaner

RAJASTHAN

Jodhpur

Jaipur

Agra

Udaipur

River

UTTAR PRADESH

NEPAL

Darjeeling

ARUNACHAL
PRADESH

ASSAM

NAGALAND

MEGHALAYA

MANIPUR

BANGLADESH

MIZORAM

TRIPURA

BURMA

Lucknow

Kanpur

Allahabad

Varanasi
(Bernares)

Ganges

BIHAR

WEST
BENGAL

Calcutta

GUJARAT

Vindhaya
Mts

MADHYA PRADESH

Ahmadabad

DAMAN
& DIU

DADRA & NAGAR
HAVELI

MAHARASHTRA

ORISSA

Bombay

Western Ghats

DECCAN
PLATEAU

Hyderabad

Bay of Bengal

ANDHRA

PRADESH

GOA

KARNATAKA

Arabian Sea

ANDAMAN
IS

Madras

Bangalore

Ootacamund

PONDICHERRY

LAKSHADWEEP
ISLANDS

KERALA

Nilgiri
Hills

NICOBAR
IS

TAMIL
NADU

Cochin

SRI LANKA

0   300 km

300 miles

5

Delhi

Delhi has been India's official capital since 1911. The Prime Minister and President both live here. The Rajya Sabha (Council of State) and the Lok Sabha (House of Commons) meet in the semi-circular Parliament House, built in 1931. It is at the top of Rajpath (King's Way), a wide road with parks on either side. To the south-west, separated by beautiful gardens, is Rashtrapati Bhavan (President's House) where India's President lives.

The Red Fort of Old Delhi, built in 1638.

The famous Pearl Mosque stands in the grounds of the fort, along with the emperor's palace and its beautiful gardens. Leading west is Chandni Chowk (Moonlight Place), a wide street built for royal processions. Nearby is the bazaar, filled with tiny stalls and shops selling gold, silver, rubies and sapphires. Incense sticks are also sold here – jasmine, sandalwood, musk and amber.

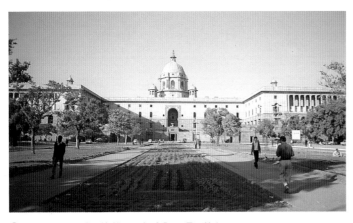

Government buildings in New Delhi.

The old city

The walled city of Old Delhi was the capital of the Moghul emperors, who ruled between 1526 and 1857. Above it lies the redstone fort built by the Emperor Shah Jehan. It is called the Lal Qila (Red Fort). Many visitors go to see the fort and enjoy the son et lumière (sound and light) show which recreates scenes from the life of the emperor.

Housing

The houses in Old Delhi are built close together and generally have four or five storeys, with a flat on each floor. Most buildings have flat roofs, from which children fly kites. When the weather gets hot, people from the flats put their bedding on the roof and sleep beneath the stars.

Between 1925 and 1947, the British built the area now called New Delhi. It was designed by the British architect Sir Edwin

Lutyens. Nowadays, the wealthy and famous live in the residential areas of New Delhi in spacious, well laid-out houses, with large gardens and separate living quarters for their servants, who would otherwise have to live some distance away in a poorer part of the city.

As industry and trade increased, factories were built on the outskirts of the capital. People drawn to the factories from other parts of the country found it difficult to pay for lodgings in the city, so they lived across the River Jamuna on the eastern outskirts of the city. This is the poorest part of Delhi, with badly built dwellings and poor sanitation.

In between are the suburbs, such as South Delhi. This is where the middle-classes live. Their houses are usually two-storey buildings, sometimes divided into two or more flats. Some people live in detached houses with small gardens.

Employment

Like most large cities, Delhi is overcrowded. People from all parts of India come here to find work in the fast developing factories. Many work as labourers or domestic servants. Others drive black and yellow taxis or motor rickshaws decorated with garlands and pictures. Women and men ride bicycles or motor-bikes to work. The well-to-do use private cars. Vehicles are vital to the business of the city but their exhaust fumes cause pollution and are carefully monitored.

Craftsmen with traditional skills such as pottery, carpet-making, weaving and wood-carving, find work easily because Indian handicrafts are popular all over the world and are in demand for souvenirs and export.

The Taj Mahal

In 1630 the fourth Moghul emperor Shah Jehan started building the Taj Mahal. It took more than twenty years to complete, and is sometimes called the eighth wonder of the world. It was erected as a tomb for the emperor's dead wife, Mumtaz Mahal, and is made of white marble, inlaid with semi-precious stones.

The Moghuls ruled northern India from almost 350 years, and built many famous palaces and monuments.

Motor rickshaws and other vehicles in a busy Delhi square.

Cities

With each passing year more people leave their villages to move to the larger cities where it is easier to find jobs in factories and industry. India's nine major cities all have more than a million people. The roads are full of cars, taxis, bicycles, trucks and motor-rickshaws, and the pavements crowded with pedestrians. Vendors selling food, sweetmeats and tea park their barrows on the roadside. Most cities are connected by road and rail and have small airports. Like Delhi, each of the three most important cities has an international airport.

Calcutta

The headquarters of the West Bengal government are in Calcutta. This is one of the most densely populated cities in the world. As an important business centre, it is very built up. In the middle of the city is the Maidan (open space). It is 3 kilometres long, with the River Hooghly on one side and Strand Road on the other. Goods are brought to Calcutta by train and road, to be carried on the Hooghly to the sea. The traffic from the jetties makes Strand Road very congested. A large underground railway is planned and should ease the traffic.

Raj Bhavan (Government House) faces onto the Maidan. The shops, cathedral and museum are to the east. The Indian Museum is one of the best in the country. In Bentinck Street is an interesting Chinese Quarter with a Chinese temple.

Calcutta is a busy, crowded city.

A view of the esplanade in Calcutta.

A slum dwelling in the centre of Bombay contrasts with modern buildings.

White buildings make Madras bright and spacious.

Bombay

Bombay is the capital of Maharashtra state. It was once a collection of seven marshy islands filled with coconut palms. By the nineteenth century much of the land had been reclaimed from the sea, cotton mills and public buildings had been put up, and the docks had been constructed. Today Bombay is the biggest of ten major ports in India. It handles mainly dry cargo and petroleum products, as well as one-fifth of India's total port traffic. It has a population of over 6 million.

Malabar Hill is one of India's most expensive residential areas with its Hanging Gardens. Downtown, in the poorer parts of Bombay, there are many high-rise apartment blocks where hundreds of people live huddled together. The less fortunate live on the streets, begging for food by day and sleeping on the pavement by night.

Madras

Madras is the capital of Tamil Nadu. It is a beautiful city with gardens and red-brick buildings. Other buildings are pure white, faced with white lime which is produced nearby. Most of the buildings are quite low, so the city looks very different from Bombay and Calcutta. The Governor's residence, Guindy Park, is set in a deer park and surrounded by three and half hectares of flower gardens. The Peoples' Park has eleven artificial lakes, sports-grounds, tennis courts and a band-stand. Somehow the pace of life also seems much slower than in other large cities. Several of India's most famous schools of classical dance are in Madras, which is known as a centre of the arts.

9

Villages

The great Indian leader Mahatma Gandhi said 'India lives in her villages . . .'. By this he meant that the traditions of India survive better in the countryside than in the cities. In spite of widespread modernization this is still true.

Villagers

Most villagers are farmers. They either farm their own land or work for a local landlord. Those who are not farmers run shops and cafés or follow the trade of their forefathers. Every village has its goldsmiths, weavers, potters and cobblers. Women do the housework, take clothes down to the nearest ghat (washing-stream), and gather firewood and cowdung for fuel. They take meals to their husbands in the fields and during harvest, help with the crops.

Village schoolchildren sit on bare earth.

If there is no piped water, laundry is often washed by hand in the river.

Women and children attending a village health centre.

The most respected people in the village are the landlord, the priest and the school-teacher. They are the ones to whom the villagers turn in times of need. They usually belong to the Panchayat (village council) which consists of respected members of the community. The Panchayat acts as an informal law court, hearing complaints and finding solutions.

The landlord, usually the head of the council, is the most powerful man and the largest employer in the village. The priest is a key figure in village life. Villagers attend the mandir (temple) regularly with an offering of food or money. Teachers are highly respected because they are guides to knowledge and good citizenship. Children obey them more readily than their own parents. Village health centres provide immunization and prompt attention to medical problems. So the population has increased in spite of widespread use of birth control.

Housing

Wealthier villagers have large and solidly built houses. But most people have a small, detached house with just two rooms. One is used for cooking and the other for sleeping. Food is cooked in metal pots over an open fire. Rush matting, cotton sheets or rugs cover the floor and furniture is usually limited to a few low stools and tables. Tin trunks are used instead of wardrobes, and hooks instead of kitchen cupboards. Some people have beds in the second room. Most families prefer to sleep on mattresses which can be rolled up and stored away, so that the room can be used for other purposes during the day. Most houses have a porch and walled yard where chickens, goats and cows are kept.

About 43% of India's 500,000 villages now have electricity and running water. But most villages still have at least one well which supplies daily needs such as cooking and bathing.

Entertainment

When all their chores are over, people gather in the square to talk, or watch television or films on government-installed screens. At weddings and festivals, they dress in colourful garments and perform traditional dances. Travelling players visit from time to time and put on plays, mostly based on the story of Rama and Sita.

Learning a trade

Some sons continue in their father's trade. Many others go to the nearest city to earn more money. Often they leave their parents, wives and children behind and send a large part of their salary home. A few leave for further education. The most popular professions are medicine, engineering and agriculture. When qualified, these fortunate ones usually return to their village to use their skills on behalf of their community.

A shepherd leads his flock through a village.

Farming

India is an agricultural country. Nearly 75% of the people live in rural areas and are connected with farming in some way. The 'green revolution' began in India forty years ago when the government decided to grow enough food for its people.

Canals and dams

The first step towards this goal was to irrigate as many places as possible, and especially those areas where there is little or no rainfall. The government started to build canals. One of the most important is the Rajasthan canal which will be 650 kilometres long when completed. It will water the rainless districts of Ganganagar, Bikaner and Jaisalmer. Another scheme, the Hirakud dam across the River Mahanadi in Madhya Pradesh, is the longest dam in the world – 5 kilometres. It waters literally millions of hectares.

Research and development

Research centres have been set up all over India to find ways of improving crops and helping farmers. They employ more than one million people, and the government sends trained officers to advise farmers on new methods. It also gives farmers grants to modernise their farms.

India manufactures its own fertilizers and pesticides. They are sprayed onto fields by light aircraft built specially for the job. Being harmful to the environment, the use of both chemicals is strictly controlled.

Rice

More than 500 million people in India eat rice every day, and it is grown by more than 25 million farmers all over the country. The best way of farming and processing rice is still by hand. The seedlings are planted in flat seed beds. When the plants turn yellow

Rice is still planted mainly by hand.

Rice paddies under cultivation in Mysore.

the crop is ready for harvesting. The pickers have to bend low to pick it by hand. Next the rice is threshed (the grain is separated from the plant) by bullocks, which trample out the grain. Finally the paddy (rough rice) is milled to remove the coarse outer husk, and dusted clean. It is now ready for packaging. Long-grain rice and Basmati rice are the most famous types grown in India.

Wheat, tea and sugarcane

Wheat, grown in Haryana, Punjab and the western regions of Uttar Pradesh, is a winter crop. It is made into flour and used to bake many different types of bread which are eaten all over India. Haryana is one of the richest agricultural regions of India. The farms are thoroughly modern and very large. Machines do the ploughing, sowing, reaping and threshing.

Tea is grown in three hilly areas – the upper valley of Assam, Darjeeling, West Bengal and the Nilgiris, South India. Indian

Workers in Gujarat gather the cane harvest.

tea is famous all over the world and is one of its major exports.

Sugarcane, one of India's most important crops, grows in Haryana, Uttar Pradesh and Bihar. Cane juice is used to make sugar, which India exports. Other traditional exports include jute, rubber, tobacco and coconut.

Women picking tea on a plantation in the Nilgiris.

India's 1894 Forest Policy allowed the rural and tribal populations to live off forest resources. Forests were cut down and replaced with crops. The Forest Protection laws passed in 1952 changed this. The forests are now preserved to protect the environment from dust, storms, winds, erosion and floods. Cow-dung and farm waste are used for fuel instead of firewood, and farming is carefully controlled. Sixty per cent of all hilly areas and 20% of the plains are to be preserved as forests.

Power and industry

India mines a number of important minerals including iron, manganese and bauxite ore, copper, mica, asbestos, sulphur and uranium. Many of these are exported as raw materials. The industrial heart of the north-east is around Calcutta. Raw materials are easily available here and there are many factories because electricity and power are in good supply. Occasional problems occur with domestic power supply everywhere.

Iron and steel

The Indian Steel Authority is one of the world's biggest industries. Iron and steel are needed to produce a great many things. Iron-ore is one of India's largest exports. India has eight big iron and steel processing factories.

They provide the raw materials for railway engines and rolling stock. India makes all the equipment it needs for its enormous railway system.

In addition, motor cars are made in Calcutta, Bombay, Madras and Bangalore, while buses, trucks, motor-bikes and jeeps are made all over the country. India is the second largest producer of scooters in the world. Aeroplanes of many kinds are manufactured in Bangalore, Hyderabad, kanpur, Lucknow and Nasik. They are made from aluminium which comes from bauxite ore. They include jetfighters, trainer aircraft, transport planes and small aircraft used for spraying crops. Commercial aircraft are still imported.

A car factory in Bangalore.

Task forces of children help with afforestation and soil conservation to lessen damage caused by industry and mining. Power plants, oil refineries, textiles, steel and sugar mills can cause major pollution. More than half the large and medium industries have installed pollution control devices to combat this. Environment protection is now built into all industrial plans. Fly-ash (waste) from factories causing water pollution is recycled into construction blocks while suitable vegetation stablises ash-dumps.

Other major industries

India has a very large ship-building industry. Ships are built in Vishakhapatnam and Cochin. Tugs and dredgers are made in Calcutta, and Goa builds ships for the navy.

India is the world's largest producer of cotton yarn with an output of one million kilogrammes a year. Mills in Bombay, Ahmedabad, Madras, Coimbatore, Calcutta and Kanpur manufacture cotton textiles, exported as ready-made clothes, soft-furnishings and household linen. The weaving industry provides work for nine million people. Small electrical items like kitchen gadgets, videos and televisions are made in India. Importing these items is discouraged through the levy of high duties or taxes.

A woman spins wool for carpet weaving. Textiles are one of India's biggest exports.

Zuari agro-chemical plant. It produces fertilisers for India's 'green revolution'.

Power

India's most important source of power is water. This is partly because electricity harnessed from water is quite cheap. It is called hydro-electric power (HEP). There are several dams for HEP in India. The most important are the Bhakra and Nangal projects in Himachal Pradesh, and the Hirakud dam, Madhya Pradesh. Bharat Heavy Electricals Limited produces the fifth largest power supply in the world. India also helps neighbouring countries with its hydro-electric projects.

India produces enough coal for all its needs. Coal is mined in West Bengal, Bihar and Madhya Pradesh. The Bengal and Bihar mines produce high quality coal, which is used to heat water and produce steam. Oil, another source of power, is drilled in Digboi, Assam, Kalol and Ankaleshwar in Gujarat, and in the Bombay High field beneath the sea near Bombay. India produces one-third of the oil it needs. The rest is imported from Middle Eastern countries. India refines its oil in Assam, Bihar and Gujarat.

Sports and entertainment

Indian films are shown in Africa, Canada, Britain and the United States – in fact wherever there is an Indian population. Non-Indian audiences enjoy them in Egypt, Iran and the Middle and Far East. Some Indian films are made for international audiences. The director, Satayjit Ray, is well known in the west.

India has the second largest film industry in the world. Of the 940 films produced each year, about a sixth are Hindi. Most of the others are Bengali, Gujarati, Marathi, Punjabi or the South Indian languages. In recent years videos have become popular so people watch films at home. This means that the cinemas do not do such good business as they used to.

India was among the first countries to make films, soon after they were invented in 1896. At first they were silent, but when sound recording was invented in the late twenties, the talking picture was introduced. Today Indian films are mostly musicals. Film songs are India's pop songs, and appear regularly in the hit parades. Snatches of these songs can be heard in the streets, barbers' shops, restaurants and markets. India's top woman singer, Lata Mangeshkar, has sung more songs than anyone else, and is in the *Guinness Book of Records*.

The film stars

Most film stars live in Bombay, the heart of the film industry. Others live in Delhi, or the South, the other homes of important film studios. It is not unusual for film stars to make three or four films at once. Some film stars become very popular and fans will often walk many kilometres to see films starring their favourite actors and actresses. Well-established stars are often voted into Parliament or State Assemblies and have successful political careers. People trust them because they feel they know them through films.

A still from the famous film "Jewel Thief" (1967), starring the actress Vyjayantimala (centre) and Dev Anand (left). Vyjayantimala is now a member of Parliament in Tamil Nadu and runs a number of classical dance academies.

Sports

The Indian Olympic Association was set up in 1927, although an Indian, Norman Pritchard, had already won the 200 metres silver medal in 1900 in Paris. In 1928, the Indian hockey team went to the Amsterdam Games where they won the gold medal for the first time. They kept it until 1964 except for one year in 1960 when they lost it to Pakistan in Rome. The First Asian Games in 1951 were hosted by India and the Ninth Asiad was held in India in November 1982.

Two hockey teams contest in India's Nehru Hockey Tournament.

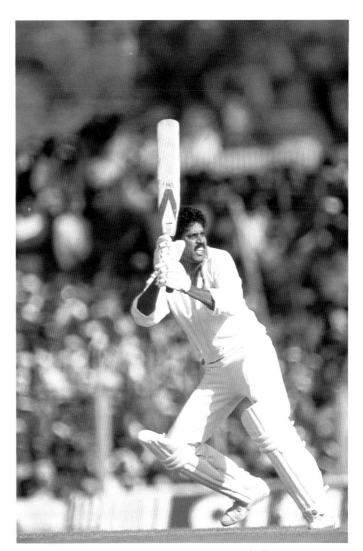

India's famous cricket all-rounder Kapil Dev.

Games from India

Two very different games were given to the world by India. Polo, rather like hockey on horseback, is played by two teams, each of four mounted men. A ball, about the size of a croquet ball, is struck with a mallet. The game originated in Persia, but soon became established in India. British officers in India adopted the game, and it is now played in many countries, including the USA and Argentina.

Snooker, a variant of billiards, was invented in 1875 in Jubbulpore, India, by Neville Chamberlain, a British officer.

But the sport for which India is most famous is cricket. The Indian cricketer 'Ranji', ruler of Navanagar, was well known in the thirties. India wins matches against strong teams such as England and the West Indies. India is also very well-known for its polo-playing princes. Among them is Colonel Bhawani Singh, who used to be the ruler of Jaipur. He often plays with the Prince of Wales. Indian women have participated in the Olympic Games since 1952. The Women's Hockey Team is strong and has won against many countries.

17

Religion

For thousands of years India was invaded by people from different lands. They introduced new ideas and customs. The Aryans from Central Asia were especially influential: their beliefs formed the basis of Hinduism, the most widespread religion in India today. From the seventh century, the Arabs, Afghans and Turks brought Islam to India, and from the fifteenth century European traders and missionaries brought Christianity. So Indians today belong to many different religions. Nearly 82% are Hindu, 11% are Muslim, and 7% are either Christian, Sikh, Parsi, Jewish, Buddhist or Jain. Buddhism and Jainism began in India but are now widespread in other countries. Both religions were started by young men from princely families who preached that all people are equal and should live in peace.

Hinduism

Hindus believe in the Supreme Spirit, Brahma, the eternal origin and final home of everything that exists. He works through three gods (the Trimurti), one of whom shares his name: Brahma, the creator, Vishnu the preserver, and Shiva the destroyer but also generator of new life. Vishnu is believed to have enjoyed a number of incarnations, of which Krishna is one of the most popular deities today. There are many other lesser Hindu gods. Mandirs (Hindu temples) are found all over India. They are often colourfully decorated and some, such as the Golden Temple of Varanasi, are very famous. Many Hindus have a prayer room, or pictures of gods, in their homes and pray to them everyday. Poorer Hindus worship in the temples.

The many different faiths of the Indian people have enriched each others' customs and way of thinking for centuries. Sadly, religious differences do sometimes turn into riots and a lot of people are killed. Though they can occur between any of the many religious groups, these disputes occur mainly between Hindus and the largest religious minority, the Muslims.

Hindu cave carvings tell the story of Shiva.

Hindus believe that when people die, their soul comes back to earth in a new form. This new form may be better or worse than their previous life – it all depends on how they have behaved. Hindus pray for help to be good, so that they will not be reborn in some lower category of life.

Islam

Muslims believe that there is only one God. Their holy book, as revealed to the prophet Mohammed, is the Koran. Five times a day, the faithful turn towards Mecca and pray They also worship in mosques. Some Indian mosques, such as the Jama Masjid in Delhi, are world famous for their beauty.

The Golden Temple at Amritsar, holy place of the Sikh religion.

Sikhism

Guru Nanak, the founder of Sikhism, lived between 1469 and 1539. He preached that there is only one God. Originally his followers were mostly tradesmen and farmers. But in 1699, they formed a group called the Khalsa in order to protect themselves against prejudice and injustice. Nowadays, most Sikhs still wear the five Ks: kes (long hair), kangha (comb), kirpan (sword), kara (steel bangle) and kaccha (short trousers). The Sikhs' holy book is the Guru Granth Sahib, and their holiest Gurdwara (Sikh temple) is the Golden Temple at Amritsar.

Christianity

Small groups of Christians are scattered all over India, with larger communities in South India – particularly in areas such as Goa, which was once Portuguese territory, and Pondicherry which was originally French. Some Christians in South India claim that St Thomas the apostle visited India and converted them. Churches and communities of various Christian orders are found all over India.

Muslims flock to the Jama Masjid mosque, Delhi.

Food

Indians are very fond of snacks. People can be seen eating during the morning, late afternoon and evening in smart hotels, cafés and fast-food chainstores. They can choose from western dishes or Indian snacks, such as vegetables fried in batter, chick peas, and yoghurt and lentil dishes. There is always a queue at the food stalls, where food is served in fresh banana leaves or in bowls made of dry leaves held together by twigs.

The rupee, made up of 100 paise, is India's official currency.

Sometimes food is bought from cheap roadside cafés and barrows. People usually take it home, or eat it in their cars. They offer a selection of meat dishes and fried savouries, which are usually very spicy and hot. Street vendors also sell a delicious range of fresh fruit juices.

Expensive restaurants make their food less spicy to suit visitors, and they serve well-known favourites. These include meat, poultry, fish, and bread baked in special underground ovens known as tandoors. Biryani (rice cooked with meat or chicken) is on every menu, and so is korma (meat or poultry cooked in spices and yoghurt). Indian sweets are very rich. They are usually made with plenty of ghee (a type of butter), creamy milk, pistachios, cashew nuts and almonds.

A Delhi food stall selling hot food.

Markets all over India sell fresh vegetables.

Religion

India is such a large country with so many religions, that there are many differences between the food of one area and another. In Gujarat for example, much of the food is made from vegetables, beans, pulses and grains, because many Gujaratis are vegetarians. Some Hindus eat meat, though not beef, and Muslims are fobidden to eat pork. As a result, beef and pork are rare in India. Lamb and chicken, on the other hand, are available everywhere.

The coastal regions

The people of West and South Bengal eat plenty of fish and rice. The food tends to be spicy, and contains lots of ground chillies. South Indians enjoy a variety of delicious foods made from steamed or fried rice. They also like coconut and sour fruits such as lemon, lime and tamarind.

Gujarat, Rajasthan and Saurashtra

Traditionally the food in these areas is served on large, round trays made from silver, copper or brass. These are called thals. Small silver bowls are placed on the thal containing meat, grain, vegetable, pulse and lentil dishes; there are also saucers containing bread and rice. On special occasions the thal is covered with a red cloth trimmed with gold.

The Punjab

The people of Punjab are hearty meat-eaters. They like large quantities of plain, wholesome food, with plenty of milk and bread made from maize, millet and cornmeal, as well as from wheat. The bread is sometimes eaten with ghee and potatoes, lentils or a regional speciality made of mustard leaves and washed down with buttermilk. It is followed by fresh, warm lumps of fudge-like confection called gur.

Here is a simple Indian recipe you can try.

Coconut (or almond) Barfi
¼ cup (2oz) water
½ cup (4oz) sugar
1 cup (scant) desiccated coconut or 1 cup ground almonds
1 cup whole dried milk

1. Dissolve the sugar in water over heat.
2. Draw off heat when dissolved.
3. Add coconut (or ground almonds) and dried milk to syrup.
4. Stir vigorously with a wooden spoon until well mixed.
5. Turn the mixture out onto a flat surface. (It should be the consistency of soft, sticky dough.)
6. Mould or roll into a slab and leave to cool.
7. Cut into square or rectangular shapes.

21

The Ganges

The Ganges (Ganga) is India's most famous river. It is 2500 kilometres long from its source in the Gangotri glacier to its delta in the Bay of Bengal at Calcutta. Two hundred million people live in its basin. It is the holy river of the Hindus, so millions of pilgrims travel along its course each year. Some prefer to walk, a pilgrimage which can take six years. The foothills are dotted with free rest-houses and mandirs. Buses and trains also run frequently between the towns.

Many yogis (holy men) live near the source of the Ganges. Some are believed to have special powers because they have prayed so long. They can supposedly tell the future, heal the sick and help people get rid of bad luck. It is said that some do not eat for months and survive the bitter winter of the mountains wearing only a loin cloth. This is because they practise yoga – a system of thought and exercise now famous all over the world. Many religious cities have sprung up along the Ganges. It is afloat with garlands, coconuts and bouquets which have been offered to the gods.

The blessings of the Ganges

Hindus believe that the waters of the Ganges have special powers to purify and heal. This is why people buy bottles of its water (Ganga Jal). They also believe that their sins are washed away if they bathe in its waters.

The Ganges is a great blessing for farmers, too, since it irrigates thousands of

Holy men (yogis) are a common sight near the source of the Ganges, the Hindu sacred river.

Flooding is common in the Ganges valley.

hectares of land. Its waters also yield plenty of fish, providing both food and a livelihood. Fishermen gather at night to tell of their adventures with the freshwater shark called the Gaunch, and the 2-metre long Katla fish.

Cities of God

Hardwar is the first religious city down from the source of the Ganges. Its name means 'Doors of Hari', Hari being the God who preserves the world. It welcomes millions of pilgrims each year. Nobody eats meat here and cows, which are sacred, roam freely about the streets. They help themselves to food from shops and stalls. When they are ill or old they are sent to special hospitals or rest homes for cows.

Varanasi is the most famous holy city in India. It dates back to 300 BC. It is filled with temples and religious museums. The Golden Temple of Shiva is especially famous, and has earned Varanasi the name of Shiva's City. Durga's Mandir, known as the Monkey Temple because of the monkeys which live there, is also very well-known. Varanasi is famous for its silk and brocades. Its markets echo with the sound of brass-workers making their celebrated brass goods.

Bridges and boats

At Allahabad, a railway bridge has been built across the Ganges. The pavements of the town are lined with vendors selling various goods. Young boys mould clay pots on small potter's wheels. The pots are used for food and drink and are thrown away after use.

Where the Ganges is too wide for a bridge, hundreds of boats are tethered together to make the traditional bridge of boats. Small river craft are lifted over the bridge. For larger boats the bridge has to be dismantled. Paddle steamers are used to carry goods to different areas. River transport is still the cheapest way of transporting heavy goods.

School children help monitor the quality of the Ganges water as part of the Ganga Action Plan. They spread information about river pollution through youth volunteer schemes, exhibitions, eco-camps and films. The Plan aims to stop domestic waste and sewerage getting into the Ganga by diverting it to treatment plants and recycling it as energy to run them.

Children are also helping to meet the target of 'greening' hectares of wasteland per year. Schools, small farmers and women's groups have set up small nurseries in rural and urban areas particularly on industrial wasteland.

Devout Hindus bathe in the Ganges at Varanasi.

Mountains

One-sixth of India consists of mountains. They run along the northern borders of the country, and line the eastern and western coast of the Deccan peninsular which forms South India. The Vindhyas divide the peninsular from the rest of India. Once trade was difficult because of the mountains. Today they are threaded with railways and roads, making cross-country travel easier.

Himalayas

The Himalayas stretch 2500 kilometres from East to West. They are the highest mountain range in the world. They are made up of three groups of mountains which run alongside each other: the Himamadri (Greater Himalayas), the Himachal (Lesser Himalayas) and the Siwalik (Outer Himalayas). Their southern slopes are in India. Mount K2 is the highest peak in India, rising to a height of 8611 metres.

Being so high, and also long, the Himalayas form a wall between India and the rest of Asia. In the old days, trade was only possible through two mountain passes: the famous Khyber pass and the Bolan pass. Roads have been built now, but travel is still difficult. The best way to go is by jeep or landrover. Adventurous tourists climb up on mules led by guides on foot.

The eternal snows of Kanchenjunga part of the Himalayan chain, seen from Darjeeling.

In mountainous Kashmir girls make their way to school.

The Ghats

The Sahyadris (Western Ghats) line the western edge of the Deccan plateau. They are 1600 kilometres long and 1200 metres high. They form a barrier between the fierce monsoon rains and the Deccan peninsular, so the plateau hardly has any rain while the coastal plains get so much that the Malabar coast is famous for its rice cultivation. Fishing is an important industry on the western coast.

The Sahyadris are rich in forests of teak, sandalwood, rosewood and ebony. The Great Indian Hornbill and the giant squirrel live here. Both are protected species.

The Nilgiris

These hills are in Tamil Nadu. They are also known as the Blue Mountains because they are covered in a blue mist and eucalyptus trees which give them a silvery-blue look.

The Nilgiris are very different from other ranges. They are rounded and covered in grass, ferns, flowers and trees. Their climate makes them perfect to live in. Streams flow through their soft slopes, spilling into hundreds of little waterfalls.

Hill stations

Ootacamund, in the Nilgiris, is a popular holiday resort. Its weather is very like English weather, and for this reason the British chose Ooty, and other hill resorts all over India, in which to spend their summers. These mountain resorts are called hill stations. Other well-known stations are Simla, Mussoorie and Mount Abu.

Roads to the hill stations are well-developed and shopping centres cater for most daily needs of visitors and residents. Clothes, books, food and gifts are easily available. Many people have holiday homes in the hills and most well-known boarding schools are located here.

Steep foothills in Uttar Pradesh.

Trains

India's favourite form of transport is the train. About 10 million people travel each day on India's 11,000 trains. You can imagine how crowded the cheaper carriages get! First-class and luxury carriages are usually quite comfortable but have to be booked weeks in advance. Some are air-conditioned others are fitted with ceiling fans. Second-class air-conditioned compartments, though less private, are also very popular. They are small curtained cubicles fitted into every available space in the carriage including the corridor. Toilets and showers are located at both ends of each carriage. As most journeys last overnight, travellers carry bed-rolls; some order food in advance to be collected at the next station.

Steam trains like this one in South India are usually very crowded!

Railway stations in India often suit the character of the city. In Varanasi, for example, the station is built to resemble a temple. Bombay Central and Victoria Terminus in Bombay are enormous echoing halls. They are so crowded that it is difficult not to bump into people. While waiting for their trains, some travellers stretch out in sleeping bags on the platform, while others open up their 'tiffin carriers' (stacked bowls held together with a metal band) and have a meal. Drinks, fruit and cooked food can be bought on most platforms. Vendors hop on and off between stations supplying passengers while the train is moving.

Large trains

India manufactures all it needs for its locomotives – whether steam, electric or diesel – at three factories: at Chittaranjan near Calcutta, and in the suburbs of Madras and Varanasi. High speed diesel trains provide efficient shuttle services as well as long-distance runs between all major cities. These are gradually replacing the old, slow, steam locomotives. Sometimes they get so crowded that people have to sit in the luggage racks. Others travel in any available space such as corridors, the floor space between seats, and the tiny areas outside the toilets.

The imposing Victorian front of Madras station.

A narrow-gauge train en route to Darjeeling.

people have to sit in the luggage racks. Others travel in any available space such as corridors, the floor space between seats, and the tiny areas outside the toilets.

An enjoyable part of any train ride is the constantly changing scenery: mountains, plains, deserts and seemingly endless stretches of green fields. Children play or swim in streams and rivers while adults till the fields or pray in temples.

'Toy trains'

Enchanting, brightly-painted trains carry passengers up to hill stations such as Simla, Darjeeling and Ootacamund. They are called 'toy trains' because they are small and slow. These tiny steam engines are so old that in other countries they can only be seen in transport museums! Unlike larger trains, toy trains run on narrow-gauge railways.

The highest station in India is at Simla. It is about 2300 metres high. The view from the train as it climbs the mountain is breath-taking. The rivers, mountains and cultivated fields look like a scene from fairyland.

Novelty railways

Until about forty years ago, important people such as governors and princes travelled in their own handsomely decorated railway carriages. These were equipped with everything their wealthy passengers needed, including radios, paintings, kitchens and bars. Private carriages were attached to scheduled trains.

Jodhpur is one of three famous cities in Rajasthan, where tourists go throughout the year. (The other two are Udaipur and Jaipur.) When the maharaja (ruler) of Jodhpur saw how interested the visitors were in his palace and family, he decided they should be able to visit Jodhpur in his family's private train. Now the royal train runs regularly from Jodhpur to Jaisalmer, packed with tourists.

A former maharaja of Gwalior was so fond of trains that he built himself a railway track for the table in his state dining room. Each rail car carried a separate dish and stopped in front of each guest before moving on. The present maharaja uses the miniature railway at parties even today.

Wildlife

India has more than a hundred wildlife sanctuaries and national parks where animals can graze and breed in safety. Some of the money needed to create them was donated by European children who gave their pocket money to the Indian Wildlife Fund. Watch towers have been built inside the parks for visitors to observe the animals, and guides take guests on tours in special buses. In some parks, visitors go sightseeing on the backs of elephants.

The tiger and the peacock

The tiger is India's national animal. Once there were 40,000. Now between 4,500 – 6,000 live in reserves and sanctuaries across the country. Tigers were killed by villagers who poisoned them in order to protect themselves and their livestock. Tiger skins

The tiger, India's national animal.

fetched a good price. Others died because their environment was damaged as a result of forests being cut down to build new settlements. Health programmes such as the prevention of malaria resulted in the death of prey and tigers started to die of starvation. Today tiger hunting is banned. Entire villages have been moved to safe areas where it is no longer necessary to use harmful methods of protection and the natural habitat is being restored.

India's national bird, the peacock, is found all over India. It is easily recognised by its enormous multicoloured tail feathers, which it spreads out in a fan when courting the much less colourful pea-hen. In Rajasthan, peacocks are very tame and wander through the villages in large flocks, helping themselves to grain, seeds and grass. Their feathers are collected and made into circular fans which are sold to tourists.

Animals of India

The magnificent white tiger is found only in Rewa, Madhya Pradesh. Its snowy pelt is striped brown or grey. Human settlement, agriculture and poisoning endanger the surroundings and prey of many animals including the snow leopard from the North Indian mountains and the Asiatic lion which survives in the Gir Sanctuary of Gujarat West India. The Grey Wolf and the Dhole (Red Dog) too, are unlikely to survive in the wild,

Langur monkeys in Khanna National Park.

so packs of them live in protected areas. Wildlife conservation workers hope that it will one day be possible to release the animals back into the wild.

The thamin deer of Manipur, the Nilgiri tahr (ibex), and the great Indian bustard of Jaisalmer, are other species of animals and birds found only in India.

The Red Panda, also known as the cat-bear, lives in the Himalayan forests between Nepal and Sikkim. It is smaller than the Tibetan panda and has a long, ringed tail. It

Elephants grazing in the Periyar sanctuary in South India.

is said to make a good pet, unlike the black or brown bear.

India has many snakes, including the largest venomous snake, the King Cobra or Hamadryad (4 metres), and the smallest, the Krait, only a few centimetres long. The snake most often used by snake charmers is the Indian cobra (2 metres).

Major game sanctuaries

Thirty-one different species of animal live around the vast Periyar lake in South India. The elephants are the most numerous. Visitors watch them while rowing on the lake, or from inside the guest house on the island.

Sanctuaries in north-east India shelter the one-horned rhinoceros, wild elephant and buffalo, white tiger, black leopard and the handsome gold langur.

The largest water-bird sanctuary in the world is in Bharatpur, near Delhi. It welcomes around 320 species of birds each year from around the world. Some flamingoes come here, but most go to the Great Rann in the Kutch peninsular where thousands of birds lay their eggs in baked mud nests. When the chicks hatch, the barren desert is alive with pink birds. This area has been nicknamed Flamingo City.

"Jungle Book" was written by Rudyard Kipling who lived in India for a long time and spoke some Hindi. He called most of the animal characters in the story by their Hindi names. *Bhalu* is the Hindi word for bear, *Sher* is a tiger, *Hathi* means elephant, *Bandar* means monkey, *Nag* and *Nagim* are the male and female cobra.

Jim Corbett also wrote about his experience with Indian animals in his books "My India" and "The Man-eaters of Kumaon".

India in the world

India became independent in 1947, and a republic in 1950. The two public holidays celebrated by all Indians, regardless of religion, are Independence Day (August 15) and Republic Day (January 26). India remains in the Commonwealth.

The past

For thousands of years people from other countries came to India, attracted by its wealth. They included Aryans, people from the middle east, and Europeans. Each group left its mark, but two groups were particularly influential. The Moghuls, during their 400 years of rule, built many gardens, palaces, forts and mosques. Gradually their art forms blended with the Indian, and developed into a uniquely Indian style. The British, during their two centuries of rule, introduced railways to India, and a variety of styles of building. Many streets, museums and parks still bear English names, such as the Victoria and Albert Museum in Bombay. One of the most lasting influences left by the British is the

A cobbler plies his trade in Jaisalmer.

English language, which is still the official language in some states, and is widely spoken throughout India. They also left behind the political system of democracy.

What India gave the world

While India has been host to many cultures over the centuries, she has also given a great deal to the rest of the world. Buddhism, which began here, has spread to Tibet, China, Japan and south-east Asia, Indian

India's national flag.

thought and philosophy has also influenced western attitudes. Yoga, now very popular in America and Europe, began in India as a form of meditation which teaches body control. Skilful use of yoga can cure aches and pains, and other health problems such as migraine.

Indian art is admired in many countries. Indian painting, sculpture, jewellery and books are among the oldest on record.

India has always been connected with the rest of the world through trade. It began to send its cotton, silk, spices and perfumes to Rome, Greece, China and Arabia more than 2500 years ago. In the seventeenth century the diamond mines of Panna (now exhausted) were visited regularly by the French jeweller Jean-Baptiste Tavernier. One of the most famous diamonds in the world is the Koh-i-Noor (Mountain of Light) which came from India. It is now one of the British crown jewels and is kept in the Tower of London. Today India is an important exporter of tea, coffee, leather goods, iron, steel and handicrafts. Indian rugs and carpets are popular all over the world.

Crowds watch a performance of the Hindu epic, Ramayana, on an open-air stage.

Bombay, the main port of the second most populated country in the world.

India's place in the modern world

As the second most populous country in the world, India has long had a very special place in world politics. It is by far the largest Commonwealth country and is recognised by major powers, such as China and Russia, as an important neighbour.

India has a land frontier of some 15,200 kilometres and a coastline of about 6000 kilometres. The borders are protected by the Indian army and navy, which are very modern and well-equipped. Most defence equipment is manufactured in India. Thirty-one laboratories have been set up for defence research. The Indian Space Commission at Bangalore, and other space centres have launched their own satellites and are involved in surveys of earth resources. The space programme is part of India's plan to improve communications, education and natural resources.

Index and summary

Area:	3,287,782 square kilometres
Population:	850,000,000
Capital city:	Delhi
Main cities:	Bombay, Calcutta, Madras, Hyderabad, Varanasi (Benares), Ahmadabad, Bangalore
Provinces:	Andhra Pradesh, Assam, Bihar, Gujarat, Haryana, Himachal Pradesh, Jammu & Kashmir, Karnataka, Kerala, Madhya Pradesh, Maharashtra, Manipur, Meghalaya, Nagaland, Orissa, Punjab, Rajasthan, Sikkim, Tamil Nadu, Tripura, Uttar Pradesh, West Bengal
Union Territories:	Andaman & Nicobar, Arunachal Pradesh, Chandigarh, Dadra & Nagar Haveli, Delhi, Goa, Daman & Diu, Lakshadweep, Mizoram, Pondicherry & Mahe
Main Exports:	Textiles, tea, iron ore, jute
Main Imports:	Petroleum, wheat, machinery
Longest river:	Ganges, 2506 kilometres
Highest peak:	K2, 8611 metres
Languages:	Hindi, English, Assamese, Bengali, Gujarati, Kannada, Kashmiri, Malayalam, Marathi, Oriya, Punjabi, (Sanskrit), Sindhi, Tamil, Teluga, Urdu
Currency:	100 paise to one rupee
National airline:	Air India